Echoes of the Unspoken

Echoes
of the Unspoken

Poems by Wayne Dodd

The University of Georgia Press

Athens and London

© 1990 by Wayne Dodd
Published by the University of Georgia Press
Athens, Georgia 30602
All rights reserved
Designed by Betty P. McDaniel
Set in Fournier
The paper in this book meets the guidelines for
permanence and durability of the Committee on
Production Guidelines for Book Longevity of the
Council on Library Resources.

Printed in the United States of America

94   93   92   91   90   5   4   3   2   1

Library of Congress Cataloging in Publication Data

Dodd, Wayne, date.
    Echoes of the unspoken : poems / by Wayne Dodd.
      p.   cm.
    ISBN 0-8203-1197-9 (alk. paper). —
    ISBN 0-8203-1198-7 (pbk. : alk. paper)
    I. Title.
PS3554.03225E25   1990
811'.54—dc20   89-37882
                    CIP

British Library Cataloging in Publication Data available

Acknowledgments

Some of the poems in this collection incorporate into themselves lines or phrases from letters from friends as well as from poems and books by other writers: Martin Heidegger, Jacques Maritain, George Oppen, Rainer Maria Rilke, Reg Saner, Charles Wright.

The author and publisher gratefully acknowledge the following publications where these poems first appeared:
Antioch Review: "Seals," "The Women"
Chariton Review: "Breakdown," "Primitive"
Context South: "Song," "On the Page," "Some First Line"
Denver Quarterly: "Hands," "Homage to Marcel Duchamp,"
   "In January," "Seasonal"
Gambit: "Imagine"
Northwest Review: "News"
The Ohio Review: "The Work," "Across Whatever Page"
Tar River Poetry: "Hylocichla Mustelina," "Desuetude"
Three Rivers Poetry Journal: Poem sequence "Echoes of the
   Unspoken," "Outside My Cabin."

Contents

I
While We Are Here

Homage to Marcel Duchamp

Not parakeets, not palm trees
                              lush in jungle air,
But the gurgle and drip rain makes
Down windows, down walls:
The constant fall
                  through the night

On roofs, on leaves, the dark
Sound of it
            in November.

On the picture postcard a man lies on his side, head
Propped on one hand, collar open, the wide smile.

Wait a minute! What's this all about? Who
Is this? What does it mean? What's on the other
                                       side?

Around us
           in the night, movements
Only the ground
                can hear: the small rivers
Of absence, the dead's
Slow turn in their dark bed.

He is relaxed, at ease.
He has nothing to do with anything.

Hands

The commonest things, my friend writes,
baffle me
I can no longer say

looking into one human
face what a person is: images the eye
each day looks into: self regarding

self in action
unpredictable improbable astonishing

the only constant
our hands
            curved still

in memory: the unique whorls
                              of expectation
imprints of nipple cheek lip, eyes

opening in the dark the light
now behind them, shapes
in the doorway becoming

ourselves: holes
                light somehow leaks away
through, cracks
              fingers touch and touch

the absence in

Across Whatever Page

To see
as well as hear it,
somehow to see

the music happen,
as when moonlight lies down
each night in the shallow graves

of footprints,
that faint hint of bones
in the outlines light

scribes across whatever page our life
faces up to, notes
we leave for ourselves

everywhere we turn:
With human beings,
Rilke says, we are in the habit of learning much

from their hands, and everything
from their face, there where light
catches, a moment, and shapes

some precinct
of trees rocks water
words, the face

of the world we take
in our hands, lines
we make in the air

to describe its presence,
the long sift of darkness into our mouths
as song

In January

As when Yo Yo Ma plays
Penderecki's Cello Concerto No. 2
the orchestra in a multitude
of voices gurgles and moans its
old griefs over the death
and imprisonment of every Czeslaw
Marek Zbigniew Andrej
Stanislaw among us their voices
rising from the ground
in wails that break up
and shiver away
through the earth killdeers
skittering along the banks
of rivers the sound
echoing in trees in rocks
deep underwater
all over Europe The
grief they play is majestic
deep sustained but of course nothing
lasts A few military
assertions on the
drums and the voices
like our lives fail again
into discord
and over all of it
passionate thoughtful brooding the cello
raises its lone voice says again
the names the losses the places
inside us and despite
the roar and clang
the engines of economics deafen us

to all harmony and balance
by still the voice
rises sometimes for a moment
out of skin and hair and wood almost
to beauty a forest
one early morning
in January the trees flocked with
something so pure so
cold we don't know how
to call it
loneliness loveliness

Hylocichla Mustelina

It starts
     with the brief runs
of a spring warbler, repeated

over and over, but sweet
and clear, like those of a coloratura
              warming up,

and, farther off, the harsh traffic sounds
crows make
     in the road.

By this time you can see
through the window the trees

in growing light detaching themselves
one by one from the dark

the forest has all night
been part of.
      Some dream

you have slept for hours
still floats above you,

like the body of your mother
now raised
     from the dead.

But like your dream the night
withdraws, finally, into its grave

and lays its tiny hands
once more along the creases

legs and torso make
together. Then it closes its eyes

and mouth and breathes
out in one long sigh

its longing
                to be touched.
And in that strange

new light again
you fail

to reach out your hand to it
as it vanishes

into the windy corners
                        of the sky
and the sealed pockets

of the earth
hands never can reach into

or fly
like that thrush outside the window

back
into the music of light from

Small Elegy

The oak sapling waves
its small arms
           for balance
in the wind, leaves

whirl up and rattle
from left to right
across the ridge. All
fall the trees

have been stripping down
for this moment. Now

against the distant shadow of
Angel Ridge the grape vines
high up in oaks let down

their tangled hair
and stream it out in the blue
rinse of air
from the north.

           Downslope
a man in a cabin
stokes and stokes the bright fire
in a woodstove, everything rushing up
into December like smoke

Outside My Cabin

now the birds
are talking softly

among themselves
supper over, their shoes off,

the woods darkening and lights
coming on in the little houses:

Comfort, the voices say,
It's been a long day,

they answer, trusting, drowsy,
the trees swaying gently

in the wind, somebody's husband
or wife already losing

the rhythm, the breathing
becoming labored,

irregular: tomorrow
as distant as China

Imagine

you are alone in a room
so quiet the only sounds
you hear are the ticks
and sighs of a wood stove
and, faint, in the distance
the passing of a train.
Maybe underneath your bed
is a secret. In the dark
you put it on, your fingers
lingering a moment
along the bill, the worn
edges. Outside the window
the white fields and black stripes
of trees rush past you
and away. The barns
and houses, the brief flash
of a window—how fast
they all rush away
into silence.
You reach your hand up
to the lever. Will anyone
hear it? you wonder.
Will anyone hear it
in time?

At Any Odd Hour of Night

It is enough to bring you suddenly
awake, the realization
that every teacher you ever had,
from kindergarten through high school, is dead, all

their small lights overwhelmed
by darkness
they could not blink away.

We are of course,
almost all of us, already
dead and live
our life together
in streets in rooms in boxes
we refuse
to be forgot in.

Consider now
a barrel of axe handles, their white-ash
curves bending the light
inside the door
of a store somewhere in Missouri,
dust rising up from the porch
with each step
of a boot.
Already you can see it
coming, the flash of a blade
near the waist,
an axe handle raised
above the small parcels:

coffee flour sugar.

Outside
clouds hover
above blackjack oaks, and wind
skitters and whirls
dust up from the road

away between the green hills.

Is this some dream
of our grandfather,
caught in the lapels of garments
we've clothed our thoughts with
all these years, or is it a story
remembered by an infant boy,
who, motherless, wandered once
into a forest
and slept

in October?

The worn floorboards that night after day
sag beneath our weight
hold all the years of our dreaming
up equally in the dark.

In the afternoon slant of light,
how the grass at your feet
flows away from you, the snake's skin moving
like unbloomed night.

In the woods, once,
your mother reached up

to a branch above the trail and in one
continuous motion in bright sun
snapped the head off
the three-foot snake she cut the air with

like a whip.

In this dream,
with your own child beside you
in the car, you stop
where a plant as large as a yucca
waves its long leaves of colors
you've never seen before: they flow
up from the center, light welling
up inside, as from an artesian spring.
This is so beautiful, so beyond imagination,
you come nearer: suddenly it
clamps itself to your leg, you tear
at the leaves, at the suction,
here on this familiar road
home, the numberless small deaths
your gullet's dark with.

In that other story,
we remember,
the boy woke and said
to the man who found him,
Cover me up with leaves, Elijah, I'm very cold.

Or unaccountably it's a dream of a troika,
night after night racing across the plains of Russia,
the blanket-wrapped message it is bearing through the night
toward someone's house
so heavy

you wake up weeping.

Or sometimes it is bears,
moving huge and dark and silent,
across that dim room you always
dream you will

wake up from

Desuetude

Countless things once held
and cared for
morning and evening
have fallen from us

into disuse
breathing out
in corners
their final sighs
of discard

Still
in sleep they come to us
again
like ghosts
of ourselves

waiting in doorways we know
we never passed through
before and repeating
strange words and names
we believe
are our own

And as if blood
and flesh were speech
we take their hands

in ours and feel
the familiar heft
and curve of bodies
answer back

such intense longing
and regret
we wake suddenly again

in dark
our beds our hands our mouths
filling up once more

with absence

What, Lasting, Comes Toward Us

> The mystery of the soul is like that of a
> closed door. When you open it, you see
> something which was not there before.
> —OSCAR KOKOSCHKA

Is and *was* have been

for one awake
or sleeping
in the rarities

of these locales
a stand of pine trees
fading steadily

toward us, needles
beneath our feet our hands
slendering up

to the light: it enters
us, becomes us,
calls out in voices

the dark
inside us quickens
to: these presences

come without warning
from hidden sources into the
hidden mind but the words

when one finds them
come from the mysterious
and universal womb

of necessity, that
sudden shadowing
of wings

All Night

it snowed,
no wind just a gentle
straight-down fall
of snow. Now
each branch and twig

holds along its top
the shaved light of January
white at all levels.

Nothing anyone says
or does is more about your life
than this: remember

the day you walked
down beside the pond
in summer, cattails
and waist-high weeds
wading the edge the bank
falling steeply away
at the far end

to deep water. Nearby
a clump of willows
throws shadows on the surface
and the silence of
the afternoon holds you

in its deep isolation.

In speargrass, in the shallows,
frogs chunk to a stop
as you walk and waterbugs
skate diagonals of solitude

in bright sun. Alone
above the sky
you look down at
in the water

you see a turtle drift slowly up
to the surface and peer out

from the other side: the slick
yellow head, the small red splashes
on the neck, your life
under the sky
always becoming

this

At Any Sudden Touch

The small wild horses
    of the mind wheel
        and rear among the bushes—

salt wind and hair and sand,
    the sharp smells
        from the sea, flaring

our eyes, our nostrils, tails
    streaming out behind
        in sunlight, waves rolling

and spilling on the shore.
    In the inlets egrets step
        and stand, white above

and below
    the spread blue
        they lower

then raise
    their heads toward.
        Now manes wave

in the wind, skin quivers
    along tensed
        legs. At any sudden

touch
    or movement they may
        wheel again and race

over blown sand,
      the only reasons
            salt wind

and hair
      and those sharp smells,
            as from the sea.

Scene, with Questions

In her light gown she comes
    in the night and bends
        over the sleepers'

bed her round arms
    bare her hands
        reaching

between them.
    Does she speak then
        in the ear

of one, touch her face
    in the mysterious dark
        with fingers

she cannot see? Her presence
    is like the night
        itself: urgent hidden

pink. Is something said
    here, some message passed
        through the disturbed air?

If she leaves
    for a moment the room
        and then returns, sliding

along the wall, will one of them cry out
    in sleep? Will either,
        waking, understand it?

II
Under Trees

Some First Line

At some point they simply
start, one or the other
of them fixing a straw
to a branch and leaving it

dangling. We look up and already
strand after strand
has been brought in
and hooked up

to the flimsy basket
they put all their eggs in
always, impermanent
and unfinished seeming

as nests gorillas
cobble together nightly
above slashed clearings: this
is the only way we ever

see it, some first line scribed
on a possible environment,
depth of field growing up
around something we become, a landscape

we know and inhabit
uncertainly, green fronds
we imagine above us
all night in the dark

Poem

The need to make a language

possible: *Make it new*
Pound said and we answer

Make it true and so
place things

in a field
hoping to catch words out a moment

in the open, their purely human
essence rising up

for an instant
out of an instant. We see them, perhaps,

in a shudder of sunlight, leaning back

toward shadows
under a tree.

Through grass through wheat through
sweet rows of corn we run
toward them, our hands raised

in light, our voices calling
into the breathing that surrounds us

names, cheeks

The Work

Say it's a spill of acorns
in the trail, each curved edge a line

between light and shade
the ground grows solid

by: *oh let not*
any absence fall

we seem to hear the voice of air
around us saying

between this full moment

and the next and already the brush
is starting its thick pull

of presence
across our life, the eternal the moment
swells into

existence as, contingency
forever shaped

in sight: the wind
that sweeps all day

the leaves, the water
that reflects
off its dark body

light
everything that is
curves into color

through: here
the trees can still

be seen, that mysterious
respiration matter

comes steadily and steadily
to mind as

On the Page

the words again become
miraculous

beings: And like all the other
creatures that fill the world

we enter through time's door
they are simply

there: They exist
body and soul

all around us—the mysterious
shapes and sounds they make

generation after century,
their long entanglements

on the earth, with each other
and with us,

the way they too
wake and dream

half in darkness half in light—

the familiar cries we make
together in the night

Song

Not only thoughts
and will we are rain

falling through
trees our hair

wet about our faces our arms
rising and falling

the rhythm our
life is

sand and wind
on our backs our legs the long

grass oh *the world*
worlds says Heidegger

white petals light
falls on like pollen

the yellow dusting
of words

on our lips our ears our throats

Echoes of the Unspoken

1.

Sometimes we dream
of Santa Barbara

in bright sun, the broad-
tailed hawks rising

inland above
the cliffs the green

stretch and roll
of the sea away

west to the islands
mist and shadow

where the goats
the mind is rut

and leap from
cleft to rise

to cleft again
in the rock hills

2.

Here

it is rain and snow and drought
and fallen leaves in sunshine reaching
all the way up

to mid-thigh: everything
incites desire
                and the slow languors
of satisfaction: pileated

woodpeckers like
pterodactyls plunge and
swoop among trees

that seem, to us,
to live forever, despite each
thrust and gouge and scratch

the world's every creature
marks its place
on the planet

by: these few
patches of light
and dark, perfumed

with smells that lift us,
in all seasons, always forward
into the present

here is

3.

As

flesh
in motion

or at rest
bones

that hold
our shapes

after we vanish
forms

we search
uncertainly

through the world
as

4.

Rain

falling through the trees
of fall for days, leaves
thick underfoot and slick

as any mucous
membrane the seasons
enter

and leave us
by:
where the buck

has scratched
the ground and sprayed
his essential

presence three
does in early
twilight gather

and fidget
beneath raked
branches: they look back

over smooth
shoulders: the long
back, the hips,

soft skin light
in the autumn
wet: in heavy air

they listen
they stamp
they switch their tails

5.

Counting

by twos
constantly

counting everything
under the sun

joined in this
rhythm

of the mind
with some other

two four six the
birds in their momentary

stop
on the earth the hickory

trees above them
around them they

fly up suddenly
in pairs

hundreds of
wings we see always

by twos becoming
one

6.

Oh

the sun shining today like time stopped
at perfection, a stillness we feel

at the center of: the bright
trunks of trees laying their straight
shadows across the ground
like exclamations: oh

the reassurance of the absolute

innocence of the elemental!
grass in the mouth, wind in the ears:

"These small nouns"

and the deer, unseen,
drifting through the woods
they imagine: silent
echoes of the unspoken: how could we not

believe this:
the skin along your wrist, your neck, legs
running straight up from the ground

like exclamations

7.

raining through the night and morning and now
    whole basketfulls of leaves dump suddenly
        from treetops

into the bright underlight and drift
    of October: through lower
        branches and leaves

still green and waving
    on their stems in light
        wind they dart

and flutter a moment
    above the earth: red
        and yellow and copper

and brown infinitely shading, the brunette
    flip and toss
        of the head

for an instant, the eyes'
    urgent message
        beneath the trees

8.

A Simple Instance

think of an oak leaf large
as a robin falling

suddenly
out of the sky

toward that
fixed goal

of 32 feet per second
per second, the invisible

air pushing
the tumbling body

back up
for an instant

then the final
quick slide

into the window
above your desk

the wild grab
at nailheads jutting out

from the wall
you plunge past

head first always
in perfect acceleration

9.

actually doing it
by hand: taking

hold of the handle
and feeling

arm join
earth wood metal

desire:
       joints
angles lines:

the difference is
becoming

girders walls rafters
the roof-peak mind

grows into: We wake
in the same moment

to ourselves
and to things

10.

So it is
in corners

where finally the eyes
fix a moment

the coming together
with what is

the crux of
our seeing

lines in
converse

the world
appearing

root and wing
in this

Seasonal

Did I mention rue
anemone
did I say blue woodland
phlox—

these glimpses
at the end of
winter thrust up
out of the ground we dream

awake, this appearing
world becoming
itself ourselves becoming
and hearing

in the silence we break
the root of our shared
being, the bright presence
we always long

to say: oh let it come, oh
let it: we
here with arms
upraised wait

III

The Phenomenology of Light

The Woman

After a sweltering night the woman
has walked out naked

among the trees
the cool air

that has rolled down
slopes down tree trunks

over rocks that look up
and down at the same time she raises

her arms her breasts

lift her waist
stretches

up and tightens light

is on her hair the curves
of her thighs beneath her
the damp

grass continues its steady

inhale exhale above her
the birds

dart and weave
and take no notice sustained
and uplifted

by the perfection
of their own
beauty

and balance above the earth

Primitive

A tree branch you have carved
And cared for, borne
By boat and plane and car
Almost the breadth

Of the continent
Just to have it
           near you

To pick up and rub

A place for your thumb

To smooth and polish
Absently

With the oils of your body,
The deep red of the heart
Wood visible
           at the ends

And all along the length
Of it, veining
To the surface

While We're Here

The sun that falls
across the grass

whatever afternoon we're here
in green

to see it
is as clear

and certain as the mind's
syntax will utter

while we're here

April

and again the trees
around us breathe

deep the air
is sweet their morning breath

is sweet the day
begins its

rachet sounds and women
get up from beds they stretch

their arms their
warm arms for an instant

they are April
again and children

their bright faces
look in on these moments

like reflections in a window

Out of Any Window

So this is the world, we say,

looking out: rain puddles
the street where robins

bustle and stop
bustle and stop, their black
head-scarves tied tight

beneath their chins: and Cézanne,
intertwining his fingers, declares

I have my motif: and all
the light the rocks hold, light that shapes

the earth's dense body

beneath us fills
some narrow lane we remember

or dream of:

where a man and a woman
rise up

from their muddy bed

apart now: their hands, their faces
awkward in the air

between them, their bent arms
still holding

the weight of this shared light

The Women

The lightning the tree holds in its side
an instant

before the overcharge of sky
splinters the air the earth the
skin and dense

flesh we stand briefly
erect as

century after century

we open our eyes and walk
forward into growing

light, mist clinging
to our feet our legs: above us

on the slope the women
all are gathered
in their generations: they reach out

their arms to us
the only sound we hear
is the sound of ourselves

breathing, the earth
breathing, they lean

toward us, mist
about their shoulders their hidden

faces
though they do not speak
as we move toward them we know

we have been called

The Return

They always came back of course

in spring, the birds
we knew

Where once we lived they flew
through the clear knowing

of our days:
the stars an apple tree
a meadow, our mothers and fathers

above us in light:

They always come back of course

in spring in spring
come back, the small heart

crashing and crashing
inside, outside
the same tall trees standing up

into the sky
like pointers

to the vanishing

Breakdown

My friend, he says, I am truly
baffled I am puzzled I am flummoxed

in the extreme: together
under the upraised hood

we stare down
into the mystery our lives

always confront
beside some highway:

even now
cars rush past us their sounds

dying away, whatever direction
they disappear in,

the private conclusion
each one right now

speeds steadily
toward: blocked lines, cancer,

a sudden loss of air
and there, always,

we are
looking down

into shadows, the failure
past mending past

understanding: we did everything
we could we tell each other,

meaning why us what now
meaning help,

and beyond the ditch the trees
above the river

darken
in the silence,

the stilled movement
of the water

Who

beside the road
today pauses, one foot raised
to rest

on a strand of fence wire,
the field beyond

bright with colors

of former horses: reds
roans buckskins browns
dappled grays blacks

Who
where wild grass
springs reassuringly

back
from another day of failing

to be true
to himself

sees possibility
only as lives gone back

to earth, their hats off
inside, coats
put away, their shoes

already heading toward beds
everything we ever dream of

is done in
—the large full curve the buttocks make
in hands, that sweet
balm, breasts

swinging down
from above or spilling
beside one: the taste

of dawn expected, horses
stepping gracefully
out of trees

into the pure morning
light

Any Morning When the Sun

comes again
across forked trees

the ancient Chinese once saw
man's very image

in, our life always
caught in branches: sun rising,

sun setting . . .
Any morning, everywhere,

when we wake,
our cupped hands

still holding traces
of the dark

sleep lowers us into
each night, the light

now beginning
to strike music

from the delicate small heads
of birds, their bright chirp

and whistle . . . Day-song,
night song: Already

everything clear
is starting up

again, no matter whose
eyes are closed

against it. Here,
pillowed up again

in stillness: the one face
each face you ever saw

was known by, its skin
smoothed and rouged and powdered,

the body's secret messages
fading and fading,

its mysterious congress
with the dark . . .

The Future

It may be no more than someone's back
glimpsed as it disappears

around a bend the curve
of its shoulders

its way of turning
toward the light may seem

familiar the trail
a faint memory

of some repeated journey
from joy to heartbreak

but you can't be sure
beyond the hills the night

has drawn its heavy drapes
across the light and the evening

airs are stoppered up
in their bright bottles

the voices of the dead are still
the voices of the dead you can't hear them

you can't hear them
no matter whose no matter when

Certain Moments

From time to time
this evening
on the forest

floor rain
strikes the broad
individual leaves

of sassafras and maple
seedlings just
this spring sprung

to light: they reel
each time and shiver

from the shock of it their
glazed surfaces
pure moments
of velocity

and mass

as color as green

underneath them steadily
the black soil darkening
with water and withdrawing

light

2.

Today the body
of a woman

who was terrified

of water seeping
over and around her

face
underground

lies cool and
dry in the lightless
air that circulates

like unheard music
around her bed

3.

I walk outside now
among the trees their
long roots

reaching down
into loam into clay
into rock

above me their tops
in wind
whip

back and forth

across the sky beyond
that mere guesswork

Crows

Is it possible that Tu Fu,
some evening beside
the river, the twilit
trees above him
full of crows, looked down and saw

beneath his feet
their disappearing

shadows? And as the sky
above him deepened and
the small boats rocked

drunkenly on the wine-
dark water did he feel
a certain pointlessness

of wings?—the earth
forever turning

us away
from light: dark
shapes we then
turn into, our arms our wings

folded tight against our bodies

News

Even after death the body
grows

The soil the air
the water that washes

over it spreads
through the earth

this news
of increase

To open up the ground
is to smell it

happening the dark
rising up

out of gravel and clay and loam
into light into breezes

trees wave their bright
scarves in and birds

sing *oh ramify*
above roots that look out like blind fish

from the hole's cut sides

O.K. Let's Suppose the Mind

forgets

how to remember
the earth

as bottom of the foot: the arms
of trees start falling

down our eyes
stop looking

up the sky
turns empty

space above us: in parallax the stars
race away

into charts into photographs: see
there it is

the out there

in circles, in grids
all around us the bare earth
makes a sound

we can't hear: the roar
the hum the scream

of energy escaping
from oil from coal from metal

hides it, its ceaseless
whisper:

at night
in our houses
of wood of brick of steel

of concrete, dreams
enter our soft
beds dogs
tear at our sides

with their teeth, surgeons
open our chests they saw

the surprised bones
in two they snip they

cut no one can hear
the sounds we are making, the small

envelope of air
inside us

around us
vanishing forever

Stormlines

Again and again this
morning's fist slams

the side of the house the trees
stretch and lean

toward windows the walls
as if responding

to their own memories
of violence

sway and turn wavy: the woman's
face below a man's

clenched hands her eyes
spread wide

as in some calendar picture a nail
no longer holds up

all its terrible events of days
now spilled

to a heap
the endless cry of voices

Seals

All night the kidneys
filter urine: the dark

blood flows back
and through, bright again
even though

we sleep, we drift

down: our eyes
are closed, elephant seals

dive several times
each hour to depths

beyond where light
vanishes
and return

to the upper world

without harm without apparent need
of rest, their great ocean

of blood breathing
for them

as they drowse, as they sink: the lungs
collapse, the permanent dark

pulses in us, pierced only by
brief flashes

whatever swims through our dreaming
brightens this black under-

sky with:
now we wake and something

rushes out of us, dives again
toward the dwindle

of sight, of thought:
we lift up our hands the stars

fly away from us:
we open our mouths the wind

whirls through them: trees
stand apart

in small groups, rocks
stare down at their feet, those indelible

tracings: the wire the searchlights
men up on towers

All Those Sharp Greens

We seem unmade

for certainty, the present's future
a sky the earth

grows bare under, trees
a mere rumor
the wind drives

through the dark:
at night, in our beds,
all the old loved smells

enter us, waft in
through some window

in the mind and there,
miraculously, they are again

in light, all those sharp greens
we breathe

together: they raise
their graceful arms once more

above us and above

vast deserts
of land of air
of water and the quiet

sounds they make
seem the voice

of the planet itself, whispering
to us, whispering

to us one last time

On Any Given Afternoon

As if from windows

framed on the ground the familiar
faces look up

toward the light the birds
above us whistle and trill and yodel

in. The green mat of their hair
at the margins, the dark centers of light
their remembered eyes are

in the earth . . . Their mouths
are closed and yet

words enter us
like song, like the presence of Being
itself, all

the lost loved voices singing out
the language of existence, its

deep warp of shadows
across the yard,
the countless

deer that move
invisibly near us

in the dense, syllabic woods

The Contemporary Poetry Series
Edited by Paul Zimmer

The Contemporary Poetry Series
Edited by Bin Ramke